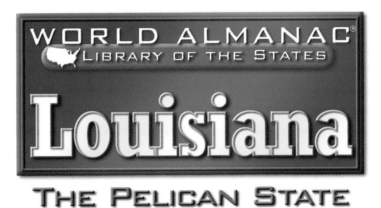

THE PELICAN STATE

by Leslie Gildart

Curriculum Consultant: Jean Craven,
Director of Instructional Support,
Albuquerque, NM, Public Schools

WORLD ALMANAC® LIBRARY

Please visit our web site at: **www.worldalmanaclibrary.com**
For a free color catalog describing World Almanac® Library's
list of high-quality books and multimedia programs, call
1-800-848-2928 (USA) or 1-800-387-3178 (Canada).
World Almanac® Library's fax: (414) 332-3567.

Library of Congress Cataloging-in-Publication Data

Gildart, Leslie S.
    Louisiana, the Pelican State / by Leslie S. Gildart.
        p. cm. — (World Almanac Library of the states)
    Includes bibliographical references and index.
    Summary: Presents the history, geography, people, politics and government,
economy, social life and customs, state events and attractions, and notable
people of Louisiana.
    ISBN 0-8368-5136-6 (lib. bdg.)
    ISBN 0-8368-5306-7 (softcover)
    1. Louisiana—Juvenile literature. [1. Louisiana.] I. Title. II. Series.
F369.3.G45   2002
976.3—dc21   2002066399

This edition first published in 2002 by
World Almanac® Library
330 West Olive Street, Suite 100
Milwaukee, WI 53212 USA

This edition © 2002 by World Almanac® Library.

Design and Editorial: Bill SMITH STUDIO Inc.
Editor: Timothy Paulson
Assistant Editors: Megan Elias and Anne Wright
Art Director: Olga Lamm
Photo Research: Sean Livingstone
World Almanac® Library Project Editor: Patricia Lantier
World Almanac® Library Editors: Monica Rausch, Jacqueline Laks Gorman
World Almanac® Library Production: Tammy Gruenewald, Katherine A. Goedheer

Photo credits: pp. 4–5 © PhotoDisc; p. 6 (top) © Corel, (bottom) © PhotoDisc; p. 7 (top) Courtesy
of the New Orleans CVB, (bottom) Dover; p. 9 © ArtToday; p. 10: Courtesy of the Library of
Congress; p. 11 © Robert Holmes/CORBIS; p. 12 © CORBIS; p. 13 ArtToday; p. 14: © Corel;
p. 15 © David J. & Janice L. Frent Collection/CORBIS; p. 17 © Joseph Scherschel/TimePix;
p. 18 © PhotoDisc; p. 19 Courtesy of the New Orleans CVB; p. 20 (all) Courtesy of the Baton
Rouge CVB; p. 21 (left) © Corel, (center) © PAINET INC., (right) © ArtToday; p. 23 © PhotoDisc;
pp. 26–27 Courtesy of the Library of Congress; p. 26 (top) Courtesy of the McIlhenny Co.; p. 27
(top) © ArtToday; p. 29 Courtesy of the Baton Rouge CVB; pp. 30–32 Courtesy of the Baton
Rouge CVB; p. 33 Courtesy of the New Orleans CVB; p. 34 (all) Courtesy of the Baton Rouge
CVB; p. 35 Courtesy of the Library of Congress; p. 36 © PhotoDisc; p. 37 © David Rae
Morris/Reuters/TimePix; p. 38 © PhotoDisc; p. 39 (top) Dover, (bottom) Courtesy of the Library
of Congress; p. 40 Courtesy of the Library of Congress; p. 41 © PhotoDisc; pp. 42–43 Courtesy
of the Library of Congress; p. 44 Courtesy of the Southwest Louisiana CVB; p. 45 (top)
© PhotoDisc, (bottom) Courtesy of the New Orleans CVB

Printed in the United States of America

1 2 3 4 5 6 7 8 9 06 05 04 03 02

Louisiana

Lively, Lovely Louisiana

Louisiana is known for a blend of European, Native American, and African cultures that make it unlike any other place. Its people feast on spicy stews and sugar-dusted beignets and move to all kinds of beats, from rollicking Cajun music to the bluesy march of a jazz funeral. Louisiana culture celebrates life in all its variety.

The sophisticated Native culture that developed in Poverty Point around 1800 B.C. made the lush area of eastern Louisiana the center of its civilization, building earthworks that rivaled the pyramids of Egypt. When Europeans arrived, they brought a mix of cultures not found in other U.S. settlements. Early French settlers brought African slaves to the colony. Both groups contributed equally to the development of Creole culture. Native Americans in the area traded with European settlers and sometimes harbored escaped slaves, further mixing cultures that could have met nowhere but in Louisiana. A strong Spanish presence in the Gulf of Mexico also had an impact on the region's way of life.

Many famous Louisianans have an air of mystery. The pirate Jean Lafitte established a secret colony for smugglers in the Gulf of Mexico. Voodoo priestess Marie Laveau was so revered that people still visit her grave for guidance. Governor Huey P. Long, known as the Kingfish, became virtual dictator of the state but was assassinated before anyone could tell how far his Louisiana charm might have taken him. Louisiana writers have often turned to the bizarre — sometimes humorously, as in the work of John Kennedy Toole, and sometimes eerily, as in the vampire novels of Anne Rice.

People who visit Louisiana never forget the state, whether they think of lazy alligators sliding through swamps, riverboats on the Mississippi, or just a great meal of crawfish étouffée. Culturally unique, Louisiana stands boldly and brightly alone, proud of its difference and welcoming to all.

▶ Map of Louisiana showing the interstate highway system, as well as major cities and waterways.

▼ The beautiful houses of New Orleans's French Quarter are decorated with wrought iron balconies.

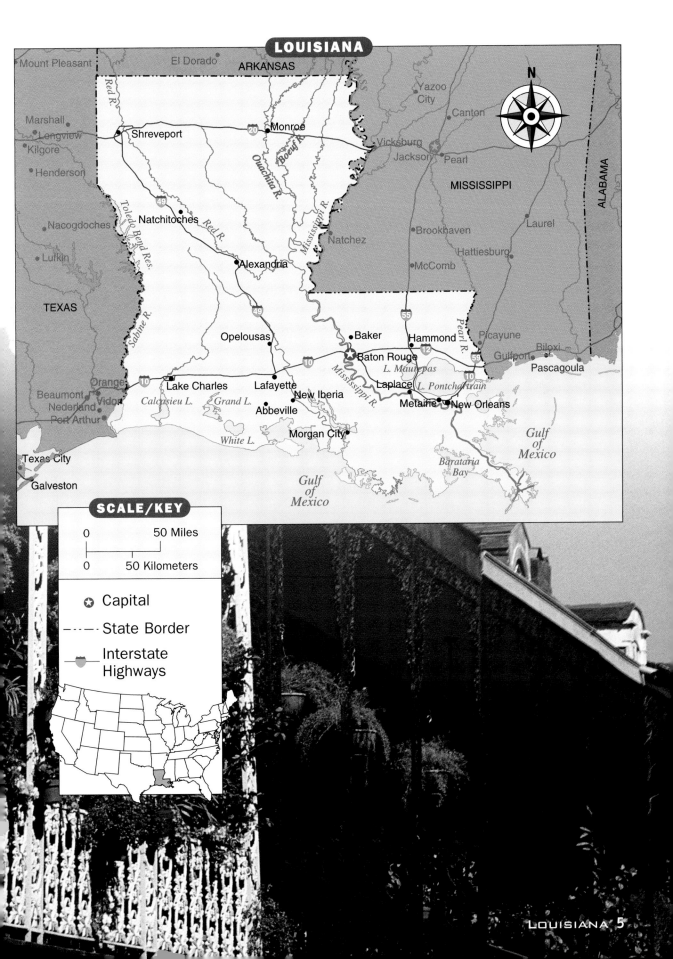

LOUISIANA

ARKANSAS

Mount Pleasant
El Dorado

Marshall
Longview
Kilgore

Henderson

Shreveport
Monroe
20

Red R.

Ouachita R.

Boeuf R.

Yazoo City

Canton

Vicksburg

Jackson
Pearl

MISSISSIPPI

ALABAMA

Nacogdoches

Natchitoches
49

Toledo Bend Res.

Red R.

Brookhaven

Laurel

Lufkin

Alexandria

Mississippi R.

Natchez

Hattiesburg

McComb

TEXAS

Sabine R.

49

I-49

Opelousas

Baker

Hammond
12

Picayune

Biloxi

Orange
Beaumont
Nederland
Vidor
Port Arthur

10

Lake Charles

Lafayette

New Iberia
Abbeville

Calcasieu L.
Grand L.

Baton Rouge

55

L. Maurepas

Laplace

L. Pontchartrain

Metairie
New Orleans

10

59

Gulfport

Pascagoula

Mississippi R.

Texas City

Galveston

White L.

Morgan City

Gulf of Mexico

Barataria Bay

Gulf of Mexico

Pearl R.

N

SCALE/KEY

0   50 Miles

0   50 Kilometers

⊛ Capital

–··–··– State Border

Interstate Highways

Fast Facts

LOUISIANA (LA), The Pelican State

Entered Union
April 30, 1812 (18th state)

Capital	Population
Baton Rouge	.227,818

Total Population (2000)
4,468,976 (22nd most populous state) — *Between 1990 and 2000, population of Louisiana increased by 5.9 percent.*

Largest Cities	Population
New Orleans	.484,674
Baton Rouge	.227,818
Shreveport	.200,145
Metairie	.146,136
Lafayette	.110,257

Land Area
43,562 square miles (112,826 square kilometers) (33rd largest state)

State Motto
"Union, Justice and Confidence"

State Songs
"You Are My Sunshine," *by Jimmie Davis and Charles Mitchell, and* "Give Me Louisiana," *by Doralice Fontane and John Croom, both adopted in 1977.*

State Mammal
Black bear

State Dog
Catahoula leopard dog — *The only dog native to the state, this hunting dog is a cross of a Native American breed and the "war dog" that the Spanish brought with them on their explorations.*

State Bird
Eastern brown pelican — *This bird scoops up fish in its large, sacklike bill.*

State Freshwater Fish
White perch — *Also known as the sac-au-lait, French for "bag of milk."*

State Tree
Bald cypress — *The bald cypress grows in many parts of the state and is especially common in swampy areas.*

State Flower
Magnolia — *The white flower is a sign of spring in the South.*

State Crustacean
Crawfish — *The crawfish, which looks like a small lobster, lives in swamps, marshes, and rivers, as well as on the state's many crawfish farms. Louisiana is the crawfish capital of the world.*

State Reptile
Alligator — *An adult male alligator can reach 12 feet (3.7 meters) in length and weigh up to 500 pounds (227 kilograms).*

State Musical Instrument
Diatonic accordion — *This instrument, commonly called the "Cajun accordion," first arrived in Louisiana with German immigrants in the late 1800s.*

Audubon State Historic Site, *St. Francisville*
Famous illustrator John James Audubon stayed at the beautiful Oakley plantation in the early 1800s. The house and grounds have been restored to their original splendor, and visitors can get a taste of what life was like on a plantation, as well as admire some of Audubon's paintings.

Los Adaes Archaeological Site, *Los Adaes*
Visitors to this archaeological dig in progress can observe while experts unearth pieces of Louisiana's rich multicultural history. Relics of Native American, Spanish, French, and U.S. exploration and settlement of the area have been found and are on display in this unique state park.

New Orleans Historical Pharmacy Museum,
New Orleans
Located in the picturesque French Quarter, this museum recreates a nineteenth-century drug store. The antique instruments and chemicals on display help visitors understand how much has changed in the practice of medicine over the past century.

For other places and events, see p. 44.

BIGGEST, BEST, AND MOST

- The state capitol building in Baton Rouge, at 34 stories, is the tallest state capitol building in the United States. It is 460 feet (140 m) tall.

- The New Orleans and Carrollton Line has been in operation since 1835, making it the oldest streetcar line in the country.

STATE FIRSTS

- **1862** The Corps d'Afrique became the first U.S. unit to have African-American officers. These troops originally were members of the Louisiana Native Guards, free African Americans who were part of the Confederate Army.

- **1905** The first U.S. off-land oil wells were located on Caddo Lake, north of Shreveport.

Marvelous Market

Every morning in New Orleans, locals and visitors alike gather at the Café du Monde on the edge of the French Market to start their day with a beignet — a deep-fried pastry heavily dusted in powdered sugar — and a cup of coffee. Louisianans make their coffee from a mix of coffee beans and chicory root, which gives it a unique, smoky taste. The French Market opened in 1791 and has been in operation since that time. It is a covered area open twenty-four hours a day, where farmers sell fresh fruits and vegetables as well as herbs, flowers, and homemade pickles and preserves. In recent years, artists and craftspeople have moved into stalls and stores near the market, adding to the liveliness of the scene.

True Love Story?

"**E**vangeline," an epic poem written by Henry Wadsworth Longfellow in 1847, depicts a love story set during the Acadian migration to Louisiana in the eighteenth century. Recently, scholars have suggested that the characters in the story were based on real people. Longfellow heard the story of two lovers separated during the migration from a clergyman, who supposedly heard it from one of his parishioners. Legend has it that the real Evangeline is buried under the corner of a church in St. Martinville. This is unlikely, however, as the Acadians of the day were all buried outside of the town. Longfellow never actually visited Louisiana.

From Cajuns to Kingfish

Though the times were full of war, the Crescent harbor presented a scene of prosperity well-pleasing to the eye.

— *Adelaide Stuart Dimitry,* War Time Sketches, Historical and Otherwise, *1909–1911*

Native Americans of Louisiana

Apalache
Attakapas
Caddo-Adais
Chitimacha
Choctaw-Apache
Clifton Choctaw
Houma
Jena Choctaw
Koasati (Coushatta)
Tunica-Biloxi

Thousands of years ago, Native Americans came to the region that is now northeastern Louisiana to hunt and fish. Archaeologists estimate that people lived in the region now known as Poverty Point between 1800 B.C. and 1350 B.C. There they built enormous earthworks, which include mounds, ridges, and trenches. Historians think that the people who lived at this site built their homes out of grass and mud on top of the ridges, which were up to 6 feet (1.8 m) high and 200 feet (61 m) apart. The Poverty Point civilization also built a spectacular bird-shaped earth mound that is 70 feet (21 m) tall and has a base that is 700 by 640 feet (213 by 195 m). At Watson Brake, a nearby site, archaeologists have discovered earthworks that are even older than those at Poverty Point, dating from 3300 B.C.

Native Americans who lived at present-day Poverty Point in northeastern Louisiana engaged in long-distance trade with people from as far away as the Great Lakes region. They imported sandstone and soapstone from present-day Georgia and Alabama, which they used to carve pots for cooking and storage. Inhabitants of the area used spears to hunt deer, rabbits, and various birds, and made flour out of nuts and acorns. They cooked their food in large, open ovens.

Although the Poverty Point settlement had been abandoned by the time Europeans arrived, Native Americans were still an active presence throughout the region. Approximately twelve thousand people, members of about thirty tribes, were living in small settlements along the banks of bayous and rivers.

DID YOU KNOW?

People who lived at Watson Brake in northeastern Louisiana made what appear to be monuments out of tons of gravel and dirt, nearly one thousand years before the Egyptians built the pyramids and long before construction began at Stonehenge. The Watson Brake Mounds required the transport of thousands of tons of soil and rock, probably in baskets and skins and probably over the course of centuries.

The Coming of the Europeans

In 1519, Spanish explorer Alonso Alvarez de Pineda reported that he had discovered the mouth of a large river that emptied into the Gulf of Mexico. This river may have been the Mississippi.

Another Spanish explorer, Hernando de Soto, encountered the Mississippi in 1541, while traveling through the southeast. De Soto died on the banks of the river in 1542.

In 1682, French explorer René-Robert Cavelier, Sieur de La Salle, was the first to reach the mouth of the Mississippi. He claimed all of the land watered by the Mississippi River and its tributaries for France, naming it *Louisiana* after King Louis XIV. In 1714, Louis Juchereau de St. Denis founded Fort St. Jean Baptiste. This was the first permanent European settlement in the region and was on the site where the city of Natchitoches now stands.

From 1717 to 1731, Scotsman John Law and his Company of the West recruited settlers and cleared land for them to live on. Law had convinced the French government to give his company exclusive rights to trade among the new colony and France and French settlements in Canada. His company also had the power to choose its own governor and to give out parcels of land to settlers. As part of the project, the company imported enslaved Africans to work on the new plantations. In 1718, Law asked Jean Baptiste Le Moyne, Sieur de Bienville, to choose a spot on which to start a town. They called the settlement Nouvelle Orléans (New Orleans), in honor of Law's friend, the Duc D'Orléans, regent of France. By 1721, there were nearly four hundred people in the town.

Refugees and Land Deals

Among those who came to the region in the eighteenth century were a group of people known as Acadians. They were descendants of French people who had settled in southeastern Canada in the early 1600s. When that territory became a British possession during the French and Indian War (1754–1763), the British government attempted to make the Acadians swear loyalty to the British king. Rather than do so, about ten thousand Acadians left. Many

▲ To mark the Louisiana territory as French, La Salle and his men erected a cross and a column carved with the coat of arms of the French king. They then sang hymns, shot their muskets into the air, and shouted, "Long live the King!" as an audience of local Native Americans observed the proceedings.

DID YOU KNOW?

Although Louisiana was explored by Europeans in the early sixteenth century, the first permanent European settlement was not established until 1714.

later returned to Canada, but about four thousand settled in Louisiana, where they developed a distinct culture that would become known as Cajun.

The Company of the West proved unprofitable for France. By secret treaty, France gave its territory west of the Mississippi to Spain in 1762, angering the French occupants of the territory when they found out. In the 1790s, a revolution in a French colony in the Caribbean called St. Domingue — now Haiti and the Dominican Republic — caused many of that colony's French-speaking settlers to immigrate to Louisiana. Spain returned Louisiana to France in 1800, and in 1803, the United States purchased the Louisiana territory from French ruler Napoleon Bonaparte. The United States bought 828,000 square miles (2,114,520 sq km) for $15 million.

At the time of the Louisiana Purchase, the area that would become the state of Louisiana was named the Territory of Orleans. William Charles Cole Claiborne was appointed governor of Orleans in 1804. He had the difficult job of adjusting a French-speaking society accustomed to the rule of a king to an English-speaking democracy. In 1809, some ten thousand more refugees arrived from St. Domingue, doubling the population of the territory. About three thousand of these immigrants were free French-speaking people of African descent. They joined an already significant population of free African Americans who lived in the territory, particularly in urban areas. In cities, slaves were often hired out by their owners and were sometimes allowed to keep a portion of the wages they earned. Some were then able to buy their own freedom. Other free African Americans in the area were the children of white slave owners and slaves.

Statehood and War

In 1812, the Territory of Orleans was renamed Louisiana and became the eighteenth state to join the Union. Claiborne was elected the first governor. The same year, the

▲ This French map, printed in the 1750s, shows the territory of Louisiana. The Mississippi River serves as a dividing line on the map, with the area to its right colored pink and all western territory colored yellow.

War of 1812 broke out between the United States and Great Britain. The Battle of New Orleans was fought on January 8, 1815, with General Andrew Jackson leading the U.S. troops, a diverse group that included pirates, Choctaw Indians, and free African Americans. This ragtag army defeated a British force twice its size, making Jackson a living legend destined for the White House. Ironically, this battle, a major U.S. military triumph, took place two weeks after the war's official end on December 24, 1814, when a peace treaty was signed in Europe. The news did not arrive in New Orleans until long after the battle.

Trade and Culture

During and after the war, settlements grew in Louisiana as trade expanded. In 1812, the first steamboat to make its way down the Ohio and Mississippi Rivers from Pittsburgh arrived in New Orleans. The towns of Alexandria, Natchitoches, and Shreveport, along with New Orleans, became important trading and cultural centers.

A culture known as Creole developed in Louisiana in the eighteenth and nineteenth centuries. From a Spanish word, *criolla*, Creole originally referred to the descendants of Spanish settlers in the Americas. In Louisiana, the term came to mean the descendants of French settlers who had intermarried with Spanish settlers. Creole society in Louisiana was proud; Creole people even spoke their own dialect of French. Related to, yet separate from, the Creole were the *gens de couleur libres*, or "free people of color," who were descendants both of white Creoles and of Africans. Some of the *gens de couleur libres* owned plantations and slaves.

Voodoo Woman

In the 1830s, Marie Laveau, a New Orleans resident, declared herself the Pope of Voodoo. Voodoo (also called Vodun or Vodou) is a religion that has its roots in Africa and was brought by slaves to the United States, where it adopted some features of Christianity. It involves rituals to win the favor of the spiritual forces that are thought to govern the natural world. Laveau, who was the daughter of a wealthy white planter and an African slave, was born either in New Orleans or in St. Domingue, probably in 1794. She worked as a hairdresser in New Orleans before devoting herself full-time to performing voodoo rituals, for which she charged money. She became highly respected as a voodoo priestess. Laveau attended Catholic mass every day, and the church gave her permission to perform some of her rituals in a space behind St. Louis Cathedral. Laveau had fifteen children, one of whom, Marie Philomene Laveau Glapion, followed in her mother's footsteps and also became a voodoo priestess. Laveau's legend lives on, and visitors frequently perform rituals at her grave in New Orleans, believing that she still has the power to help them affect the future.

The Civil War

In the 1850s, the United States was deeply divided over the issue of slavery. Heavily dependent on slave labor to support its plantation economy, Louisiana sided with pro-slavery states when they discussed separating from the antislavery Northern states.

Louisiana seceded from the Union in 1861 and was an independent republic for two months before joining the Confederacy. Between April 17, 1862, and May 18, 1864, at least twenty major Civil War battles and engagements were fought on Louisiana soil. Both the North and South fought fiercely for control of the state because whichever side controlled Louisiana controlled the mouth of the Mississippi River, an important access to trade, and New Orleans, home to some of the South's largest commercial, industrial, and financial interests.

Flag Officer David G. Farragut and a Union fleet began operations against New Orleans in April 1862. On April 24, Farragut's men destroyed the Confederate fleet that was protecting Fort Jackson and Fort St. Philip on the Mississippi River. Confederate troops in New Orleans evacuated, rather than let the city be bombed. General Benjamin F. Butler occupied the city on May 1, 1862, and from that time New Orleans served as a Union base of

▼ In August 1862, troops of the Union Army captured Baton Rouge. In the background are the warships *Winona*, *Richmond*, and *Mississippi* and, in the foreground, disheartened Confederate Army soldiers.

operations. Louisiana's Confederate government set up its capital in Opelousas in 1862 and Shreveport in 1863. African-American soldiers engaged in battle against Confederates for the first time in 1863. Some of these soldiers were former slaves who had been liberated by Union troops while others were free African Americans who sided with the Union.

▲ On May 23, 1863, 30,000 Union troops attacked a Confederate stronghold in the Battle of Port Hudson.

Aftermath and Reconstruction

The Civil War devastated Louisiana's economy. More than half of the state's livestock was killed or confiscated. The sugar industry lost close to $100 million, and the plantation economy was nearly destroyed.

After the war, the U.S. government established Reconstruction in the states of the Confederacy. Reconstruction was a project to reestablish order in the South and, in part, to secure civil rights for African Americans. Reconstruction involved stationing federal troops in the former Confederate states. Louisiana was occupied by these troops longer than any other Southern state. During Reconstruction, Pinckney Benton Stewart Pinchback, the son of a white planter and a freed slave, briefly became acting governor of the state. Reconstruction ended nationally with the withdrawal of federal troops in 1877.

Without the support of federal troops, the Reconstruction project of making a place for African Americans in the state's political life came to an end. An era of terrorism began, in which whites attacked and killed many African Americans and established laws, known as Jim Crow laws, to limit their civil rights. Despite the hardships of this period, however, a vibrant African-American culture flourished in the state, particularly in New Orleans.

Into the Twentieth Century

During the late nineteenth and early twentieth centuries, Louisiana's economy expanded from reliance on agriculture to include the petroleum and natural gas industries and the chemical industry. The late nineteenth century was notable

Freedom Rider

In 1892, thirty-year-old shoemaker Homer Plessy purposefully took a seat in a whites-only car of the East Louisiana Railroad. Because Plessy was part African American, the train conductor told him to move. Plessy refused and was arrested. In court, he claimed that his constitutional rights had been violated. Plessy was convicted and appealed his case. In 1896, the U.S. Supreme Court upheld the railroad company's right to segregate as long as it provided equal accommodations for both races. The decision is considered one of the worst in the Court's history. It was not reversed until 1954.

for the emergence of the so-called "Bourbon Democrats," who were masters of voting fraud and highly resistant to African-American civil rights. They were named after the Bourbon Dynasty of France, a regime that was famous for its resistance to change.

In the 1890s, the Bourbon Democrats were challenged by the Populists, a coalition of small farmers and laborers who wanted greater control over markets and who advocated racial integration.

In 1901, oil was discovered near Jennings, creating a booming industry. The first natural gas pipeline in the state was built in 1908 between Shreveport and the Caddo Field in northeastern Louisiana. In 1927, heavy rains caused the Mississippi River to overflow, creating what came to be known as the "Great Flood." The river remained at flood level for more than 150 days in a row.

Kingfish, Depression, and War

Perhaps the most famous episode in Louisiana's political history began in 1928, when Huey P. Long, known as "the Kingfish," became governor. Long established many public works programs. Long governed his state almost as a dictator. During his administration, however, roads were built in the state, the state university system expanded, and a new capitol building was constructed in Baton Rouge. At the same time, Long was believed to be involved in corruption. He was elected U.S. senator for the state in 1930. He continued to serve as governor, however, and didn't take his Senate seat until a hand-picked successor was installed. When Louisiana began to suffer along with the rest of the

Rushing Riverboats

In the second half of the nineteenth century, steamboats were a popular means of transportation along the rivers of the South. In 1870, a famous race from New Orleans to St. Louis, Missouri, took place between the *Natchez VI* and the *Robert E. Lee*. After the *Natchez* had set a record, making the trip to St. Louis in three days, 21 hours, and 58 minutes, the captain of the *Robert E. Lee* challenged the captain of the *Natchez* to a race. The *Robert E. Lee* won the race, probably because the captain of the *Natchez* refused to unload his cargo or passengers and got stuck on a mudflat for six hours. The *Robert E. Lee* was traveling without cargo or passengers, but only beat the *Natchez* by a few hours. Today, steamboats such as the *M.S. Natchez* (*below*) still ply the Mississippi, many carrying tourists curious about the history of these unique vessels.

nation during the Great Depression of the 1930s, Long at first supported President Franklin Roosevelt's New Deal program for rebuilding the economy. Later, Long decided Roosevelt's plans were not radical enough and suggested a program called "Share the Wealth," in which government funds would be taken from the rich and given to the poor.

In 1935, Long was planning to challenge Roosevelt for the presidency in the 1936 election when he was assassinated. His son, Russell, was a U.S. senator for Louisiana from 1948 to 1987.

The Depression was largely ended by the mobilization for World War II. During the 1940s and 1950s, the number of factories in the state grew about 60 percent.

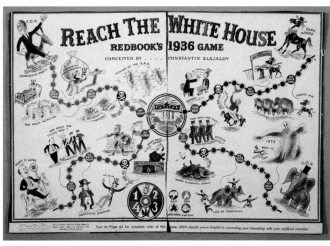

▲ *Redbook* magazine published this board game, which depicts Huey P. Long challenging Franklin Roosevelt for the presidency.

Civil Rights and the Modern Era

During the 1950s, the Civil Rights movement took hold in Louisiana. The Louisiana State University Graduate School was integrated by a court order in 1950. Although the U.S. Supreme Court declared segregation in public schools unconstitutional in 1954, Louisiana did not integrate its public schools until 1960. In 1968, Ernest N. "Dutch" Morial became the first African American elected to the state house of representatives since the days of Reconstruction. Morial went on to be elected the first African-American mayor of New Orleans, in 1977.

On the economic front, the late 20th century saw a steep rise in the number of service industry jobs within the state, as well as expanded oil and natural gas drilling. In 1988, the largest offshore structure in the world, an oil-drilling rig nicknamed Bullwinkle, was installed about 150 miles (241 km) south of New Orleans in the Gulf of Mexico.

Democrat Mary Landrieu made Louisiana history in 1997 by becoming the first woman ever elected to the U.S. Senate by the state. She is the daughter of a famous mayor of New Orleans, Moon Landrieu.

Family Business

In 1940, Hale Boggs was elected to the U.S. Congress from Louisiana. When Boggs disappeared in a small plane over Alaska in 1972, his wife Lindy was elected to replace him. She served in Congress from 1973 to 1990 and introduced legislation dealing with civil rights and equal pay for women, among other issues. Boggs, who graduated from Tulane University, became the first woman elected to the U.S. House of Representatives from Louisiana and the first to preside over the Democratic National Convention, in 1976. From 1997 to 2001, she was the U.S. ambassador to the Vatican in Rome, the first woman to serve in this post. Boggs's daughter, Cokie Roberts, is a nationally-broadcast news reporter for both ABC-TV and NPR radio. Roberts has said, "Politics is our family business."

Living in Louisiana

> He was a valiant youth, and his face, like the face of the morning, Gladdened the earth with its light, and ripened through into action.
>
> — *Henry Wadsworth Longfellow, "Evangeline"*

Louisiana has a remarkably diverse population that has often been compared to gumbo, a tasty local stew in which all the ingredients blend well together but still retain their individual flavors.

A History of Diversity

Native Americans have inhabited the state for more than five thousand years. Today, Louisiana's Native American tribes consist of Apalache, Caddo-Adais, Koasati (Coushatta), Chitimacha, Houma, Tunica-Biloxi, and various groups of Choctaw. There is also a mixed Choctaw and Apache group in northwestern Louisiana. The swamps and prairies of Louisiana sheltered the Native American cultures of the region throughout the years of white settlement, and Native people have retained much of their languages and many of their traditions. Today, approximately 0.6 percent of the state population are Native American.

Age Distribution in Louisiana
(2000 Census)

Age	Population
0–4	317,392
5–19	1,050,637
20–24	325,571
25–44	1,293,128
45–64	965,319
65 & over	516,929

Across One Hundred Years

Louisiana's three largest foreign-born groups for 1890 and 1990

■ 1890   ■ 1990

Germany	Ireland	France	Vietnam	Honduras	Cuba
14,625	9,236	8,437	11,313	8,338	4,920

Total state population: 1,118,587
Total foreign-born: 49,747 (4%)

Total state population: 4,219,973
Total foreign-born: 87,407 (2%)

Patterns of Immigration

The total number of people who immigrated to Louisiana in 1998 was 2,193. Of that number, the largest immigrant groups were from Honduras (12.6%), Vietnam (9.2%), and Mexico (6.0%).

Louisiana's Cajuns are descended from the Acadians, French settlers from eastern Canada who immigrated to Louisiana in the mid-eighteenth century when the British took control of their lands. The name *Cajun* is a corruption of the French *Acadien*, which is pronounced "Acadjunn." Today, "Cajun Country" includes twenty-two parishes (counties) and is known for its cooking, music, and language, a mix of French and English. The 1800s also brought German, Italian, and Irish immigrants to Louisiana. Most of the German immigrants were assimilated very rapidly into Creole society, even to the point of translating their names into French. African Americans have long been a powerful cultural force in Louisiana, particularly in New Orleans, where a large, free black population flourished under Spanish rule in the eighteenth century.

▲ This photograph from the 1940s shows a group of Cajun children living in rural Marksville.

Who Lives in Louisiana?

Between 1990 and 2000, the population of Louisiana grew by almost 6 percent. The majority of people in Louisiana — 68 percent — live in urban areas, most of them in the southern and eastern parts of the state, around New Orleans and

---

Heritage and Background, Louisiana   Year 2000

▶ Here's a look at the racial backgrounds of Louisianans today. Louisiana ranks third among all U.S. states with regard to African Americans as a percentage of the population.

Total population 4,468,976

White 2,856,161 63.9%

American Indian and Alaska Native 25,477 0.6%

Native Hawaiian and other Pacific Islander 1,240 0.03%

Some other race 31,131 0.7%

Two or more races 48,265 1.1%

Asian 54,758 1.2%

Black or African American 1,451,944 32.5%

Note: 2.4% (107,738) of the population identify themselves as **Hispanic** or **Latino,** a cultural designation that crosses racial lines. Hispanics and Latinos are counted in this category as well as the racial category of their choice.

Baton Rouge. The state as a whole has a population density of 102.6 people per square mile (40 per sq km). In the northern and western parts of the state, which are more rural, there are only about 30 people per square mile (12 per sq km).

Louisiana's population became older in the latter part of the twentieth century. The median age in the state rose from 32.9 in 1990 to 34 in 2000. Nationally, the median age climbed from 32.9 to 35.3.

Religion

Louisiana's population is overwhelmingly (94.7 percent) Christian, although people in the state belong to many different denominations. The largest single group, approximately 35 percent, is Roman Catholic. This reflects the state's French and Spanish heritage, as both France and Spain have been predominately Catholic for many centuries. Among other Christian denominations are Baptists, who make up about 30 percent of the state's total population. Methodists make up about 5 percent. Other groups with smaller percentages are Episcopalians, Presbyterians, and Lutherans. Among Louisianans who are not Christian, 0.1 percent of the population are Buddhist, 0.1 percent are Muslim, and 0.4 percent are Jewish. About 0.4 percent of the state's population practice Native American religions.

▼ The bright lights of downtown New Orleans, known as the Big Easy, can be seen from Algiers on the opposite shore of the Mississippi River.

Education

The first schools in Louisiana were private religious schools run by French monks around 1725. The first publicly funded school system was set up in New Orleans in 1841. Today, there are approximately 755,000 students in public schools in Louisiana. The state has the highest percentage nationwide of students who attend private schools — about 12 percent. Louisiana has a comprehensive system of public higher education, including junior colleges, four-year colleges, and graduate schools. Louisiana State University offers courses in each of the sixty-four parishes of the state and has campuses in Alexandria, Baton Rouge, Eunice, New Orleans, and Shreveport. The University of Louisiana has eight campuses, including Louisiana Tech in Ruston and Grambling State in Grambling. Among the state's well-respected private institutions are Tulane University and Loyola University, both in New Orleans.

Educational Levels of Louisiana Workers (age 25 and over)	
Less than 9th grade	372,913
9th to 12th grade, no diploma	430,959
High school graduate, including equivalency	803,328
Some college, no degree or associate degree	520,671
Bachelor's degree	267,055
Graduate or professional degree	142,068

Bayous and Backwoods

> I saw in Louisiana a live-oak growing,
> All alone stood it and the moss hung down from the branches,
> Without any companion it grew there uttering joyous
> leaves of dark Green.
>
> — *Walt Whitman*, Leaves of Grass, *1867*

Louisiana is part of the Gulf Coastal Plain, which is one of the major natural regions of the United States. The part of the state that stretches along the Mississippi is the Mississippi Alluvial Plain, known commonly as "the Delta" because it includes the delta of the Mississippi. The area tends to be flat and swampy. The western half of the state is in the West Gulf Coastal Plain, which has some hilly parts in the north and prairies in the south.

Louisiana has 387 miles (623 km) of coastline along the Gulf of Mexico. With all the bays, inlets, and peninsulas along the coast, however, the state's shoreline is actually 7,721 miles (12,423 km) long.

The Mississippi River Delta, where the river empties into the Gulf of Mexico, is an area of about 13,000 square miles (33,670 sq km). As the river water travels south, it picks up large quantities of mud, which it then dumps as it enters the Gulf. As the mud builds up, it blocks the course of the river, which periodically redirects itself to flow around the mud. The Mississippi dumps more than 640,000 cubic feet (18,100 cubic m) of mud into the Gulf of Mexico every second.

Highest Point

Driskill Mountain
535 feet (163 m)
above sea level

▼ *From left to right:* oak trees line the driveway to Oak Alley, a nineteenth-century plantation house; a cypress tree rises on the banks of a bayou; rural Cajun homes; a coral snake; cypress trees in Honey Island Swamp; Spanish moss hanging from the trees in a New Orleans park.

Louisiana's other major rivers include the Red, Ouachita, and Pearl Rivers. Southern Louisiana is known for many minor streams, called bayous, that wind through swampy areas and are home to a wide variety of wildlife, including alligators and herons. The soil of the delta region is particularly rich because of the minerals that are carried down the river and deposited there.

Climate

Louisiana is a warm and humid subtropical state. Winters are short, with temperatures rarely falling below 50° Fahrenheit (10° Celsius), and summers are long and steamy. July is the wettest month of the year, and thunderstorms are common throughout the summer. It seldom snows anywhere in the state, but it rains more than 60 inches (152 cm) in the southeast in an average year. Occasionally, tropical storms and hurricanes blow in from the Gulf of Mexico and cause serious damage to the coast. Because the Mississippi River periodically floods, Louisianans have constructed levees, which are walls that keep the river within its banks.

Plants

Nearly half of Louisiana is covered with forests, and 150 species of trees are native to the state. In the northwest and southeast, hills are covered in loblolly pine trees, as well as other evergreens. Near the Mississippi River Delta, oak, ash, and gum trees grow, and in the wettest regions in the southern part of the state, the bald cypress is common. Oak trees grow throughout most of the state and are often seen covered in Spanish moss, a grayish-green plant that drapes itself over trees. Spanish moss is not actually a moss but is related to the pineapple family. People have used it as a stuffing for furniture.

Average January temperature:
Monroe: 44°F (7°C)
New Orleans: 51°F (11°C)

Average July temperature:
Monroe: 82°F (28°C)
New Orleans: 82°F (28°C)

Average yearly rainfall:
Monroe: 67.2 inches (171 cm)
New Orleans: 61.9 inches (157 cm)

Major Rivers

Mississippi River
2,340 miles (3,765 km)

Red River
1,290 miles (2,076 km)

Ouachita River
605 miles (973 km)

Largest Lakes

Lake Pontchartrain
400,000 acres (161,880 ha)

Toledo Bend Reservoir
185,000 acres (74,870 ha)

Lake Maurepas
58,240 acres (23,570 ha)

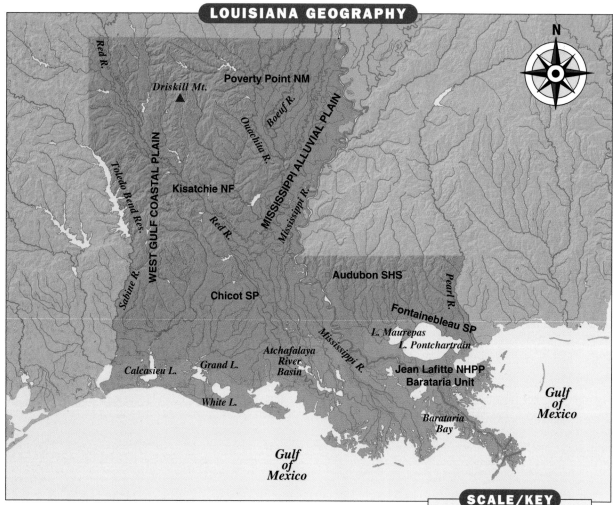

Red R.

Driskill Mt.

Poverty Point NM

Boeuf R.

Ouachita R.

Toledo Bend Res.

WEST GULF COASTAL PLAIN

Kisatchie NF

MISSISSIPPI ALLUVIAL PLAIN

Mississippi R.

Red R.

Mississippi R.

Sabine R.

Chicot SP

Audubon SHS

Pearl R.

Fontainebleau SP

L. Maurepas

L. Pontchartrain

Atchafalaya River Basin

Mississippi R.

Calcasieu L.

Grand L.

Jean Lafitte NHPP Barataria Unit

White L.

Gulf of Mexico

Barataria Bay

Gulf of Mexico

Among the wildflowers that brighten the state in the spring and summer are yellow jasmines, orchids, asters, and Louisiana irises. Flowering trees and shrubs include wild azaleas, magnolias, redbuds, and dogwoods.

Animals

Louisiana's swamps and bayous are home to a large population of alligators. These amphibian reptiles can be up to 12 feet (3.7 m) long and weigh 500 pounds (227 kg). They live in the water, spending most of the day swimming around just under the surface and sleeping in mud holes. At night, they hunt for small animals and fish. Until the mid-twentieth century, hunters killed alligators for food and for their skins, which were used to make shoes and bags. Overhunting, however, threatened to wipe out the alligator population. A careful program of conservation has increased the population, and they are no longer endangered.

Among the several kinds of snakes native to the state are coral snakes, copperheads, water moccasins, and canebrake rattlers, all of which are poisonous.

Freshwater fish (which may serve as an alligator's dinner) include catfish, paddlefish, barfish, and largemouth black bass. Crawfish (or crayfish) are also found in the rivers and streams of the state and are a main ingredient in many Cajun dishes. The Gulf of Mexico supports a wide variety of fish such as tarpon, mackerel, bluefish, sharks, and rays as well as shellfish such as oysters and mussels.

Muskrats, mink, and raccoons are among the many mammals that live in the swamps of southern Louisiana. There are also a small number of black bears remaining in the swamps, although their population has been reduced through hunting. As in many other parts of the country, white-tailed deer and gray squirrels are common in Louisiana. Present in smaller numbers are gray foxes, beavers, and otters.

Louisiana serves as the southern station of the Central and Mississippi Flyways — routes followed by migrating birds every year. Many birds migrate through the state each year, including ducks and geese. Birds that live in the state include the endangered brown pelican, the laughing gull, the blue heron, and the snowy egret. Other birds that are at home in Louisiana are woodpeckers, whippoorwills, and scarlet tanagers.

Salt of the Earth

Salt deposits left over from a narrow sea in southern Louisiana were compressed under heavy layers of sediment over thousands of years and pushed up, forming large columns. In some places, these columns rose above the surface of the earth or water, creating what are known as salt domes. Avery Island, where peppers for Tabasco sauce are grown, is a salt dome island. In many cases, huge reserves of natural gas have been found trapped within salt domes. In recent years, salt domes have been used to store oil that has already been extracted. A "bottle" is drilled in the salt column, and oil is poured into it.

▼ The snowy egret was hunted almost to extinction for its beautiful plumage.

From Hot Sauce to High Tech

> Yes, we destroy poverty by defeating ignorance.
> By educating our people, we build new
> opportunities and create new jobs.
> This we have been doing.
> — M. J. "Mike" Foster, Jr., Louisiana governor, 2001

Beginning with the French and Spanish colonization of Louisiana, the area had a thriving agrarian economy that developed into a robust plantation economy. The Civil War led to the end of the slave labor system but did not end the state's reliance on agriculture as a primary means of economic support. In the northern part of the state, cotton was the main cash crop, while in the semitropical south, sugarcane plantations were most successful. The economy remained reliant on agriculture until the early twentieth century, when petroleum and natural gas were discovered and mining grew in importance. In the second half of the twentieth century, the state became industrialized and now has a relatively diverse economy in which manufacturing, mining, trade, agriculture, and services all play a role.

Services

As has been the trend in most other states over the last twenty years, the service industry has become the largest sector in Louisiana's economy. Most jobs in this sector are in urban areas. Service industry jobs include a wide variety of positions, from doctors and lawyers to sales clerks, waiters, and bankers. Many jobs in the wholesale and retail trade, as well as in tourism, are service-sector jobs.

Agriculture

Approximately 8.1 million acres (3.3 million ha) of Louisiana are farmland. Of these acres, 65 percent are used for raising crops, while most of the rest are used for grazing

Top Employers
(of workers age sixteen and over)
Services 34.3%
Wholesale and retail trade 22%
Manufacturing . . 12.5%
Transportation, communications, and other public utilities 7.8%
Construction 6.8%
Public Administration . . . 6.1%
Finance, insurance, and real estate 5.8%
Agriculture, forestry, and fisheries 2.5%
Mining 0.3%

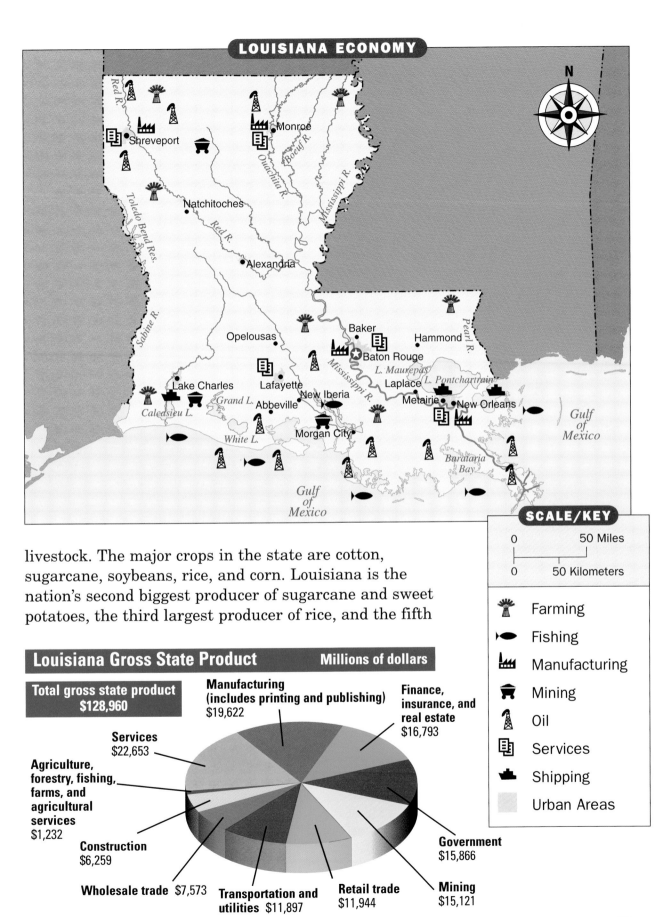

LOUISIANA ECONOMY

livestock. The major crops in the state are cotton, sugarcane, soybeans, rice, and corn. Louisiana is the nation's second biggest producer of sugarcane and sweet potatoes, the third largest producer of rice, and the fifth

SCALE/KEY

0 — 50 Miles

0 — 50 Kilometers

- Farming
- Fishing
- Manufacturing
- Mining
- Oil
- Services
- Shipping
- Urban Areas

Louisiana Gross State Product — Millions of dollars

Total gross state product $128,960

- Manufacturing (includes printing and publishing) $19,622
- Finance, insurance, and real estate $16,793
- Services $22,653
- Agriculture, forestry, fishing, farms, and agricultural services $1,232
- Construction $6,259
- Wholesale trade $7,573
- Transportation and utilities $11,897
- Retail trade $11,944
- Mining $15,121
- Government $15,866

largest producer of cotton. Among animal products, chickens and eggs are the most important. Louisiana farms also produce pecans, peaches, and hot peppers. The McIlhenny sauce company, located on Avery Island, has been producing world-famous Tabasco hot pepper sauce since 1868.

Fishing

Louisiana's fishing fleet lands approximately one-quarter of the total catch in the United States each year. Among the varieties that coastal fishing brings in are tuna, menhaden (used for fertilizer), and red snapper. No other state produces more shrimp or oysters, and millions of pounds of crawfish are taken from the Atchafalaya River Basin every year. The state has a thriving pisciculture (fish farming) industry that raises catfish as well as crawfish.

Mining

There is so much fossil fuel under the surface of Louisiana and offshore that it ranks second only to Texas in the production of natural gas. There are oil wells throughout the state and in coastal waters, but the northwestern and coastal parts of the state are where the industry is primarily concentrated.

The state also has salt and sulphur mines along the Gulf of Mexico. Salt was first mined in the area by Native Americans. Large-scale salt mining began in Louisiana during the Civil War in open pits, and the first underground mine was opened soon after in 1869.

Manufacturing

Louisiana's leading manufacturing activity is in chemical production. Chemical products include fertilizers, drugs, plastics, soaps, and petrochemicals. Petrochemicals are

Made in Louisiana

Leading farm products and crops
Sweet potatoes
Rice
Sugarcane
Soybeans
Cotton
Corn
Chickens
Eggs
Pecans
Peaches
Hot peppers
Shellfish
Fish

Other products
Salt
Petroleum
Natural gas
Coal
Chemicals
Vehicles

chemicals made from the vast amounts of petroleum produced in the state. Louisiana factories also produce vehicles for commercial use, missiles for the U.S. military, and products for the space program

Transportation

Ever since the French first settled in Louisiana in the eighteenth century, the state has been an important link in the international transportation of goods. More total tons of cargo pass through the Port of South Louisiana, in Laplace, than are handled at any other port in the United States. The Louisiana Superport, built 20 miles (32 km) off the coast of Lafourche Parish, is one of the only ports in the country that is deep enough to accommodate the supertankers that haul oil from the Middle East.

▲ The Lake Pontchartrain Causeway, the longest bridge over water in the world, carries traffic between the southern and northern ends of Lake Pontchartrain.

Tourism

Louisiana is a favorite destination for international travelers and U.S. tourists alike. Each year, more than 20 million people visit the state, 7 million of them during the Mardi Gras festivities. Tourists spent nearly $9 billion in the state in 2000 — $4 billion of that sum in New Orleans alone.

Major Airports		
Airport	Location	Passengers per year (2000)
Louis Armstrong New Orleans International	New Orleans	9,874,257
Baton Rouge Metropolitan	Baton Rouge	853,205
Shreveport Regional	Shreveport	752,290

▼ Bull Bayou Oil Field in northwestern Louisiana was a major discovery in 1913.

Pelican State Politics

> Her accomplishments during the course of a long and distinguished career stand as testimony to the true meaning of public service.
>
> — *Louisiana Senator Mary Landrieu on former Louisiana Congresswoman Lindy Boggs, 1997*

L ouisiana is unique among the United States in that its legal system is based on the Napoleonic Code, a set of civil laws, rather than on the English common law system. Common law comes from decisions judges have made as issues came up in court cases. Civil law, on the other hand, begins with a code or system of written statutes. Judges apply and interpret these laws, but judges do not make the laws. The Napoleonic Code was named for Napoleon Bonaparte, who was emperor of France, and it went into effect in 1804, the year after France sold Louisiana to the United States.

When the United States gained control of Louisiana in 1803, residents of the region, who had been used to living under the civil codes of the Spanish and French governments, resisted the establishment of new laws that were based on English traditions. Rather than just impose the U.S. system on the people of Louisiana without their consent, William Claiborne, the territorial governor, permitted a compromise. Instead of creating counties, Claiborne allowed the region to be divided into parishes, which had been the organizing units of the Catholic Church. He also allowed Louisiana (or Orleans as it was known at the time) to adopt some parts of the Napoleonic Code because the code represented the formalization of traditions with which the territory was familiar. The Civil Code of 1808 was a compromise between English and French legal traditions.

Louisiana has had eleven constitutions in its history as a state. The current constitution was adopted in 1974.

State Constitution

We, the people of Louisiana, grateful to Almighty God for the civil, political, economic, and religious liberties we enjoy, and desiring to protect individual rights to life, liberty, and property; afford opportunity for the fullest development of the individual; assure equality of rights; promote the health, safety, education, and welfare of the people; maintain a representative and orderly government; ensure domestic tranquility; provide for the common defense; and secure the blessings of freedom and justice to ourselves and our posterity, do ordain and establish this constitution.

— *Preamble to the 1974 Louisiana Constitution*

Article I of the constitution addresses the civil rights of the people in much the same way as those rights are addressed in the first ten amendments to the U.S. Constitution. The Louisiana Constitution, however, not only guarantees the right to freedom of expression but also the right to individual dignity, extending protection against discrimination because of "birth, age, sex, culture, physical condition, or political ideas or affiliations."

Like the United States, Louisiana has a tripartite, or three-part, system of government consisting of the executive, legislative, and judicial branches.

Executive Branch

The executive branch of government is charged with executing, or enforcing, the laws. The power to execute the law is the responsibility of the following elected officials, all of whom serve four-year terms: the governor, the lieutenant governor, the attorney general, the treasurer, the secretary of state, the commissioner of agriculture and forestry, the commissioner of insurance, and the commissioner of elections. The governor proposes legislation and budgets and has the power to veto legislation. The lieutenant governor is the second-in-command and also serves as the commissioner of the Department of Culture, Recreation, and Tourism. The attorney general represents the state in all legal actions. The state treasurer is responsible for keeping track of all of the state's expenses. The secretary of state keeps all of the state's records and runs several museums dedicated to state history. None of these executive officers may serve more than two terms in a row.

▼ The Louisiana State Capitol in Baton Rouge was a pet project of Governor Huey P. Long. The capitol was completed in 1932, after only fourteen months of construction, and cost $5 million to build. It is a notable example of the art deco style of architecture. Long was shot to death in the building in 1935 and buried on the capitol grounds.

Elected Posts in the Executive Branch		
Office	Length of Term	Term Limits
Governor	4 years	2 terms
Lieutenant Governor	4 years	2 terms
Secretary of State	4 years	2 terms
Treasurer	4 years	2 terms
Attorney General	4 years	2 terms
Commissioner of Agriculture and Forestry	4 years	2 terms
Commissioner of Insurance	4 years	2 terms
Commissioner of Elections	4 years	2 terms

Legislative Branch

The Louisiana State Legislature is bicameral, which means it has both a senate and a house of representatives. There are 39 members of the senate and 105 members of the house of representatives. State senators and representatives are elected to four-year terms. The Louisiana legislature convenes annually in regular session, in odd-numbered years on the last Monday in March, for no more than sixty legislative days, and in even-numbered years on the last Monday in April, for no more than thirty legislative days. Members of the legislature propose bills and discuss them in committee meetings. Once a bill has been approved by one house, it is passed to the other for review. If a bill passes both the house and the senate, it is sent to the governor. The governor can veto a bill, but the legislature can override the veto if two-thirds of the members of each house agree to do so.

Judicial Branch

Judicial power rests in a state supreme court, courts of appeal, district courts, and other lesser tribunals as provided by law. The supreme court has a chief justice, determined by seniority in years on the court, and six associate justices.

▼ The Old Governor's Mansion in Baton Rouge was built in 1930 for then-governor Huey P. Long. It was built according to Thomas Jefferson's original plans for the White House in Washington, D.C.

Four justices must agree in order to reach a majority opinion. All Louisiana judges are elected, except when they are temporarily appointed to fill vacancies. This differs from the federal system, in which judges are appointed by the president with the advice and consent of the Senate. Louisiana Supreme Court justices serve for terms of ten years.

Local Government

Parishes are the basic unit of government at the local level. The legislature can establish, dissolve, or merge parishes and allocate their property. Most parishes are governed by a group of people called a police jury, a system that dates from the state's days as a European colony. The police jury has between five and fifteen members who are elected by the residents of a parish. The jury has both legislative duties — making laws — and administrative duties, such as making budgets and negotiating contracts. An advantage of the police jury system is that juries are often large, so there is more chance for an individual juror to know some of the people she or he represents. A disadvantage of the system is that it does not provide strong central leadership. A few parishes are governed by home rule charters, which allow them greater freedom in deciding how local issues will be resolved. Home rule parishes may make their own laws as long as these do not conflict with those of the state.

▲ Architect James Dakin referred to his design for the Old State Capitol building in Baton Rouge as "Castellated Gothic." The building served as the seat of state government from 1850 to 1932 and stands on a bluff above the Mississippi River. It is now the Old Louisiana State Capitol Center for Political and Governmental History.

Party Politics

From the end of Reconstruction until the middle of the twentieth century, the Democratic party was dominant in Louisiana. When the state cast its electoral votes for Republican candidate Dwight D. Eisenhower in the 1956 presidential election, however, it became apparent that the tide was turning. In 1979, Republican David C. Treen was elected governor, the first from that party since the period of Reconstruction.

State Legislature			
House	Number of Members	Length of Term	Term Limits
Senate	39 senators	4 years	3 terms
House of Representatives	105 representatives	4 years	3 terms

Let the Good Times Roll

> New Orleans food is as delicious as the less criminal forms of sin.
> — *Mark Twain, U.S. author, 1884*

Louisiana is a place where people "let the good times roll," enjoying life and making every day special. Cajun cooking is often used as a symbol of the state's complex heritage, which combines elements of European, African, and Native American cultures. While the state is notable for this unique and lively combination, each tradition also continues to exist separately from the others, making Louisiana one of the most culturally dynamic places on Earth. From the mysterious, sweltering bayous to the wild jazz of New Orleans to the blues of the Delta region, Louisiana is seldom predictable and always fascinating.

▲ A typical Louisiana crawfish boil. The crawfish, a crustacean, is a main ingredient in many famous Louisiana dishes.

Cajun and Creole Cooking

Louisiana is famous for good food of all kinds. At cafés and restaurants throughout the state, Cajun and Creole seasonings and preparations make Louisiana cuisine special. Famous dishes include gumbo, a stew that includes seafood and okra, and jambalaya, a rice dish made with peppers, seafood, and sausage. Étoufée is a spicy sauce containing shrimp or crawfish. Cajun and Creole cooking became widely popular in the United States in the 1980s, and Paul Prudhomme, a Louisiana chef, became one of the most famous cooks in the nation. Several Cajun and Creole restaurants in New Orleans have been in existence since the late 1800s. Bananas Foster, a desert of flaming bananas over ice cream, was invented at Brennan's in New Orleans in 1951 by Chef Paul.

Good Rockin'

In the late 1940s, New Orleans musician and singer Roy Brown recorded a song called "Good Rockin' Tonight." It was the first song that used the word *rock* to describe the style that would later be called rock and roll. Louisiana's musicians, such as Antoine "Fats" Domino, helped develop the style.

Dancing in the Streets

Mardi Gras is a long, joyous, and very public party that takes place each year in New Orleans and other Louisiana cities, such as Mamou and Lafayette. As soon as Mardi Gras ends, people begin preparing for the next one. Mardi Gras — French for "Fat Tuesday" — is a celebration of life that takes place before the Christian period of Lent, a time of repentance and abstinence. Fat Tuesday, also called Shrove Tuesday, is the day before Ash Wednesday, when Lent begins. Mardi Gras festivities in New Orleans start on January 6, the twelfth night after Christmas, with masked balls. During the two weeks before Fat Tuesday, the streets are filled with gorgeous, elaborate parades. Parade floats carry "krewe" members, who belong to social clubs and who throw doubloons (pretend money), beads, and other items to the people along the streets.

Music

New Orleans musicians have had a tremendous impact on twentieth-century music. Jazz was born in the city's saloons and in the music of its famous brass marching bands that play in Mardi Gras parades and funerals alike. One of the pioneers of jazz, "Jelly Roll" Morton, was born in New Orleans and became famous as a ragtime piano player.

Fit for a King

A very popular custom in Louisiana during Mardi Gras is the making of a "king cake," which represents the legend of the three kings who brought gifts to the infant Jesus. A baby doll is baked inside the king cake, and, according to tradition, whoever gets the piece of cake with the baby in it must throw the next party.

▼ Each Mardi Gras "krewe" chooses a theme for its floats. Krewe members then spend the better part of a year designing and building these elaborate structures.

Louisianans enjoy a full range of cultural events throughout the state, from the formality of the Baton Rouge Symphony (*left*) to the casual good times of a Cajun accordion concert (*inset*).

Louisiana blues artists were among the earliest to make records, influencing all of the rhythm-and-blues artists that followed. In and around the major cities of New Orleans and Baton Rouge, great rhythm-and-blues traditions still prosper today. Blues legend Huddie "Leadbelly" Ledbetter's final resting place is just west of Shreveport. Ledbetter, who wrote "Goodnight Irene" and "Midnight Special," grew up entertaining in Shreveport's St. Paul's Bottoms, now known as Ledbetter Heights.

Cajun and zydeco are forms of music that began in the swamps and bayous of southern Louisiana, with their roots in Louisiana French-Acadian culture and African folk music. Cajun music uses the fiddle, the accordion, and a "tit fer," or iron triangle, struck with a spike to provide rhythm. It is dance music, whether a two-step or a waltz, and the lyrics are always in French. Zydeco arose from a Creole musical tradition, called "La La," enjoyed by African-American farmers in the southwestern region of the state. Zydeco artists use accordions and washboards to blend La La with American rhythm and blues. More recently, a new sound — "bounce" — has emerged, which is a fusion of rap and brass-band jazz.

Louisiana also has a long tradition of supporting classical music. In 1796, the first opera performed in the United States opened in New Orleans. Since then, opera and symphony orchestra music have been a constant feature of

Louisiana Folk Medicine

A form of nontraditional medicine is practiced in the Acadian regions of Louisiana. *Traiteurs* — meaning "treaters" in French — heal through prayer. *Traiteurs* are expected to practice according to a strict set of canons, or rules. The canons include prohibitions against advertising one's services and accepting thanks or payment of any kind. There can be no body of water between the healer and the patient. Power is always passed from an elder person to a younger person, and many believe that it must pass from a man to a woman or from a woman to a man.

cultural life in the state. There are several orchestras, including the Louisiana Sinfonietta and the Louisiana Philharmonic Orchestra.

Museums

Many of Louisiana's museums are dedicated to celebrating the history of the state and its people. The Cabildo in New Orleans was built to house the Spanish government of the city and is now part of the Louisiana State Museum. Exhibits in the Cabildo include a rich assortment of artifacts from the state's history. Museums such as the New Orleans Historical Pharmacy Museum, the Louisiana Cotton Museum in Lake Providence, and the Louisiana State Oil and Gas Museum in Oil City give visitors a glimpse into the state's past, from the daily life of its residents to the growth of its economy.

Celebrating the state's present and future, the Contemporary Arts Center in New Orleans is a showcase for multimedia works by local and international artists.

In Shreveport, the Louisiana State Exhibit Museum is itself a work of art. The building, which was designed in 1937, is on the National Register of Historic Places. Among the diverse wonders of its collection are an impressive exhibit of ancient Native American objects, a 49-foot (15-m) relief map of the state, and a group of dioramas made of beeswax.

Many of the grand houses of the plantation era can be found in a region known as "plantation country," which stretches along the Mississippi River in an area between the Atchafalaya Basin and Lake Maurepas. Visitors may tour many of the old houses and stay overnight in some. Among the famous plantation houses are Magnolia Mound, Greenwood, and The Myrtles, which is rumored to be a haunted house. The River Road African American Museum at the Tezcuco Plantation houses a collection of art and artifacts related to the lives of African slaves who worked and lived on the plantations during the period before the Civil War.

The Arts

Louisiana's rich cultural heritage includes the works of great writers such as Kate Chopin, whose stories of Cajun and Creole life became famous in the late nineteenth

▲ Louisiana author Truman Capote (1924–1984) became famous as a writer when he was in his early twenties. His major works include *Breakfast at Tiffany's* (1958) and *In Cold Blood* (1966), both of which were made into hit movies. Capote was known for his stinging critiques of the New York jet set in the 1960s and 70s, particularly with such nonfiction works as *The Dogs Bark: Public People and Private Places* (1973).

century. Walker Percy's and John Kennedy Toole's tales of New Orleans can be both bizarre and hilarious. Writers from the state have often turned to the violent and macabre for subject matter. Anne Rice, who is perhaps the most well-known of Louisiana authors, writes novels about creepy subjects such as vampires and mummies, while Truman Capote is sometimes called the father of the true-crime genre. James Lee Burke's mysteries are set in southern Louisiana and are full of local color. Poet Arna Bontemps was another Louisianan who used literature to create powerful portraits of his community. His life and work are celebrated at the Arna Bontemps African American Museum in Alexandria, his birthplace.

The Grand Outdoors

There are lots of interesting places to visit in Louisiana. Many private companies offer swamp tours, and some thirty state parks offer access to the diverse beauties of the state's wilderness. Chicot State Park is the largest state park, with more than 6,400 acres (2,590 ha). Its rolling hills are covered in dense forest and are ideal for hiking, while Lake Chicot is a delight for canoers and sports fishermen.

The Kisatchie National Forest in north-central Louisiana consists of 600,000 acres (242,820 ha) of land divided into six separate pieces. Some sections have rocky hills for vigorous hiking, although none is higher than 400 feet (122 m). The Kisatchie National Forest has something for everyone, with

Louisiana Vocabulary

Atchafalaya: \uh-CHAFF-uh-LIE-uh\ n. a wetland in southern Louisiana

bayou: \BUY-you\ n. a small, slow-moving river

beignet: \ben-YAY\ n. a fried donut that has no hole in the center

boudin: \BOO-dan\ n. a Cajun meat-and-rice sausage

chank-a-chank: \CHANK-a-CHANK\ n. Cajun music

cochon de lait: \ko-SHAWN-da-LAY\ n. a pig roast party

étouffée: \AY-too-FAY\ n. spicy sauce containing crab, crawfish, or shrimp

▼ Louisiana bayous are a paradise for professional fishermen as well as for people who fish for fun.

campgrounds, lakes, and more than 100 miles (161 km) of trails for hiking, biking, and horseback riding.

Many of the state's parks and national historic sites are both educational and recreational. At Poverty Point National Monument, visitors can marvel at the giant earthworks built by the region's early Native settlers. In the Barataria Preserve (part of the Jean Lafitte National Historic Park and Preserve), just across the river from New Orleans, there are 8 miles (13 km) of walking paths through the swamp and forest and 20 miles (32 km) of rivers for those who would rather explore by boat.

Along the northern shore of Lake Pontchartrain, Fontainebleau State Park surrounds the ruins of a plantation sugar mill, offering visitors historical information as well as a lovely beach and picturesque picnicking and camping spots.

At the Audubon State Historic Site at Oakley Plantation in St. Francisville, visitors can see the place where the famous illustrator John James Audubon worked on thirty-two of his pictures of local birds. The plantation, where Audubon served as a tutor in 1821, has been restored to give visitors a glimpse into the daily life of an early nineteenth-century plantation. The main house, separate kitchen building, slave quarters, and formal and kitchen gardens are all open to the public. Visitors may also view some of the works that Audubon created while he lived at the house.

Sports

Louisiana has only one major league professional sports team, the New Orleans Saints. The Saints have not yet won a Super Bowl, but they have won two National Football Conference West titles and have appeared in five playoffs since 1985. The Sugar Bowl, one of the most important events in college football, is held every year in New Orleans on New Year's Day. The winner of the Sugar Bowl is considered one of the top college teams in the nation.

New Orleans was once home to a National Basketball Association (NBA) team, the Jazz, but this team was relocated to Salt Lake City, Utah, in 1979.

▼ The New Orleans Saints football team gets its name from a famous jazz song, "When the Saints Go Marching In." The team plays its home games in New Orleans' famous Superdome.

Louisiana Luminaries

My greatest instinct is to be free.
I found that in New Orleans.
— *Tennessee Williams, U.S. playwright (1924–1984)*

Following are only a few of the thousands of people who were born, died, or spent much of their lives in Louisiana and made extraordinary contributions to the state and the nation.

JEAN LAFITTE
PIRATE

BORN: *circa 1780, probably France*
DIED: *circa 1826, possibly Mexico*

Jean Lafitte was a privateer — someone whose private ship is authorized by the government to attack other ships. He was also a pirate and smuggler. Some Latin American countries, which were rebelling against Spain, hired Lafitte's ships to attack Spanish boats and steal whatever goods they were transporting. Lafitte and his brother then sold the goods, which included slaves, from their base on several islands in Barataria Bay. During the War of 1812, the British tried to hire Lafitte to help them seize New Orleans. They offered him money, land, and a commission in the British Royal Navy. Lafitte pretended to consider the offer but instead warned U.S. General Andrew Jackson about the British plans. Lafitte and his pirate band then fought alongside the U.S. troops in the Battle of New Orleans. After the war, they went back to smuggling and attacking Spanish ships, eventually moving to Mexico. No one knows for certain when or where Lafitte died.

LOUIS MOREAU GOTTSCHALK
PIANIST AND COMPOSER

BORN: *May 8, 1829, New Orleans*
DIED: *December 18, 1869, Tijuca, Brazil*

Louis Moreau Gottschalk began playing piano at an early age. A member of Creole society, he was exposed to the music of the Creoles by his grandmother and nurse when he was still a child. At the age of thirteen, he went to Paris to study composition and piano. There, he established his reputation as a composer and pianist. Gottschalk was one of the first American musicians to have an international music career. His incorporation of Creole folk music and Caribbean styles into his own compositions was innovative and thrilled audiences. Although he spent his short life touring Europe and the United States, performing his pieces, Gottschalk always considered New Orleans his home.

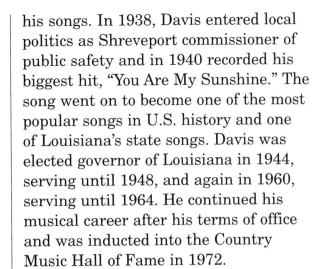

JIMMIE DAVIS
GOVERNOR AND MUSICIAN

BORN: *September 11, 1899, Quitman*
DIED: *November 5, 2000, Baton Rouge*

James Houston Davis grew up in a two-room house with ten brothers and sisters. The family was very poor but valued education, so Davis worked his way through college at Louisiana College and graduate school at Louisiana State University. He worked as a teacher and a court clerk, all the while also performing as a singer and guitar player. In the 1930s, he made several records, and more famous artists, such as Bing Crosby and the Andrews Sisters, began recording his songs. In 1938, Davis entered local politics as Shreveport commissioner of public safety and in 1940 recorded his biggest hit, "You Are My Sunshine." The song went on to become one of the most popular songs in U.S. history and one of Louisiana's state songs. Davis was elected governor of Louisiana in 1944, serving until 1948, and again in 1960, serving until 1964. He continued his musical career after his terms of office and was inducted into the Country Music Hall of Fame in 1972.

LOUIS ARMSTRONG
MUSICIAN

BORN: *July 4, 1900, New Orleans*
DIED: *July 6, 1971, New York, NY*

Louis Daniel Armstrong grew up in poverty in New Orleans and went on to become one of the most popular musicians in history. Armstrong got his nickname, "Satchmo," because he had a very big mouth and friends called him "satchel mouth," which was then shortened. When he was fourteen, Armstrong was sent to live in a home for juvenile delinquents and, while there, learned to play the cornet. Music

became his passion, and he performed in jazz bands in New Orleans. Armstrong (*left*) is widely recognized as one of the most important musicians of the twentieth century, having influenced not only other trumpeters and cornet players but also, directly or indirectly, nearly all jazz music. He helped pioneer swing, which later formed the basis for most rhythm-and-blues music, and he was known for the joyfulness he brought to his playing and singing.

LILLIAN HELLMAN
PLAYWRIGHT

BORN: *June 20, 1905, New Orleans*
DIED: *June 30, 1984, Martha's Vineyard, MA*

Lillian Hellman is considered one of the most important playwrights in U.S. history, having written eight original plays and four adaptations, two of which received New York Drama Critics Circle Awards. She also wrote three memoirs, articles for national magazines, and several screenplays. Her best-known plays were *The Children's Hour* (1934), *The Little Foxes* (1939), and *Toys in the Attic* (1960). Hellman, whose writing attacked injustice and evil in many forms, became a target of the House Un-American Activities Committee (HUAC) in the 1950s and was blacklisted, meaning that people were told not to hire her or work with her. She was the companion of mystery writer Dashiell Hammett, who also was attacked by the HUAC. Hellman's book *Scoundrel Time* (1976) was a fierce criticism of the HUAC.

MICHAEL DEBAKEY
HEART SURGEON

BORN: *September 7, 1908, Lake Charles*

Michael Ellis DeBakey graduated from medical school at Tulane University in New Orleans in 1932 and earned a master of sciences degree there in 1935. DeBakey served with the U.S. Surgeon General's office during World War II and helped create mobile army surgical hospitals, or MASH units. After the war, DeBakey worked on ways to repair human heart valves. He found a way to use plastic tubing to replace blood vessels and invented a device that could be put into a chest to help a person's heart pump blood. Today, DeBakey is chancellor emeritus of the Baylor College of Medicine in Waco, Texas. He has performed more than sixty thousand heart surgery procedures in his lifetime and has trained thousands of surgeons in these techniques. DeBakey was given the National Medal of Science in 1987 and has won numerous other awards.

MAHALIA JACKSON
GOSPEL SINGER

BORN: *October 26, 1911, New Orleans*
DIED: *January 27, 1972, Evergreen Park, IL*

Mahalia Jackson began singing in church at the age of five. She was also inspired by female blues recording artists such as Ma Rainey and Bessie Smith, although her very religious family did not approve of this kind of music. In 1932, Jackson began touring with the Johnson Gospel Singers, possibly the first professional touring gospel group, but by the middle of the 1930s she had established herself as a solo act. Completely devoted to gospel music, Jackson refused to perform any other kind of music. She became world-famous for her powerful voice and joyful delivery, playing sold-out concerts at Carnegie Hall in New York City and singing at the presidential inauguration of John F. Kennedy in 1961. She was active in the Civil Rights movement and was a close friend of Dr. Martin Luther King, Jr. She sang "I Been 'Buked and I Been Scorned" on the steps of the Lincoln Memorial in Washington, D.C., in 1963 just before he gave his famous "I Have a Dream" speech.

FATS DOMINO
MUSICIAN

BORN: *February 26, 1928, New Orleans*

Antoine "Fats" Domino grew up in a family of musicians, speaking French. His brother-in-law, who was a professional guitarist, taught him how to play piano, and he gave his first public performance when he was ten years old. Domino dropped out of school at the age of fourteen so that he could work in a factory during the day and play piano in clubs at night. In 1949, he recorded his first song, "The Fat Man," about a voodoo god of good luck. Domino had many hits, including "Ain't That a Shame" (1955) and "Blueberry Hill" (1956). One of the pioneers of rock and roll, he was inducted into the Rock and Roll Hall of Fame in 1986 and won a Grammy Award for Lifetime Achievement in 1987.

ANNE RICE
AUTHOR

BORN; *October 4, 1941, New Orleans*

Born Howard Allen O'Brien, Anne Rice changed her name to Anne when she was in the first grade. She spent her childhood in New Orleans and Texas and went to college in San Francisco, California. When she was twenty, she married poet Stan Rice. She wrote her first novel after the death of her five-year-old daughter, Michele. The book *Interview with the Vampire* became an instant best seller. Rice wrote four other very popular books about vampires. In 1988, Rice moved into a Victorian mansion in New Orleans, which she used as the setting for several books about witches. She has also written historical fiction, including *The Feast of All Saints*, about African-American Creoles in the nineteenth century.

WYNTON MARSALIS
MUSICIAN

BORN: *October 18, 1961, New Orleans*

Wynton Marsalis is the son of noted New Orleans jazz pianist and teacher Ellis Marsalis. Wynton began playing the trumpet when he was six and gave his first public performance when he was seven. When he was fourteen, he gave his first professional performance with the New Orleans Philharmonic. Marsalis played with the New Orleans Civic Orchestra while he was still in high school. He attended Julliard School of Music in New York, before joining Art Blakey's Jazz Messengers, a famous band. Marsalis signed his first record contract at age nineteen. He became known for his strict allegiance to classic jazz, and he became the first musician ever to win Grammy Awards for both jazz and classical records in the same year. In 1997, Marsalis won the Pulitzer Prize for his composition *Blood on the Fields*. His brothers Branford and Delfeayo are also musicians.

Louisiana
History At-A-Glance

1682
René-Robert Cavelier, Sieur de La Salle, claims Louisiana territory for France.

1714
Louis Juchereau de St. Denis founds Fort St. Jean Baptiste, the first permanent European settlement in Louisiana.

1718
New Orleans is settled by the Company of the West.

1762
France gives Louisiana territory to Spain, regaining it in 1800.

1803
The United States purchases Louisiana Territory from France.

1804
William Charles Cole Claiborne is appointed governor of the Territory of Orleans.

1808
Civil Code of law is established.

1812
Louisiana becomes the eighteenth state to join the Union.

1815
Andrew Jackson defeats the British at the Battle of New Orleans.

1838
New Orleans celebrates Mardi Gras for the first time.

1847
Henry Wadsworth Longfellow publishes "Evangeline," his epic poem about an Acadian romance.

1861
Louisiana secedes from the Union.

1600 **1700** **1800**

1492
Christopher Columbus comes to New World.

1607
Capt. John Smith and three ships land on Virginia coast and start first English settlement in New World — Jamestown.

1754–63
French and Indian War.

1773
Boston Tea Party.

1776
Declaration of Independence adopted July 4.

1777
Articles of Confederation adopted by Continental Congress.

1787
U.S. Constitution written.

1812–14
War of 1812.

United States
History At-A-Glance

1862
New Orleans is captured by the Union.

1877
Reconstruction Period ends following the 1876 election of U.S. president Rutherford B. Hayes.

1901
Oil is discovered near Jennings.

1927
Poydras levee is dynamited to protect New Orleans from flooding.

1935
Huey Long is assassinated at the state capitol building in Baton Rouge.

1950
Louisiana State University Graduate School is integrated by court order.

1975
The Louisiana Superdome opens in New Orleans.

1977
Ernest N. "Dutch" Morial is elected first African-American mayor of New Orleans.

1980
David Connor Treen takes office as the first Republican governor in more than one hundred years.

1984
The Louisiana World Exposition brings millions of visitors to New Orleans.

1987
Russell Long retires after thirty-eight years as U.S. senator for Louisiana.

1992
Hurricane Andrew strikes southern Louisiana.

1800 — **1900** — **2000**

1848
Gold discovered in California draws eighty thousand prospectors in the 1849 Gold Rush.

1861–65
Civil War.

1869
Transcontinental railroad completed.

1917–18
U.S. involvement in World War I.

1929
Stock market crash ushers in Great Depression.

1941–45
U.S. involvement in World War II.

1950–53
U.S. fights in the Korean War.

1964–73
U.S. involvement in Vietnam War.

2000
George W. Bush wins the closest presidential election in history.

2001
A terrorist attack in which four hijacked airliners crash into New York City's World Trade Center, the Pentagon, and farmland in western Pennsylvania leaves thousands dead or injured.

▼ The town of Lake Charles, shown here in 1923, was established as a major port after a deep water channel was created in 1926, linking the town to the Gulf of Mexico.

Festivals and Fun for All

Check web site for exact date and directions.

Angola Prison Rodeo, Angola

Since 1965, prisoners at the Louisiana State Penitentiary have been competing against each other each October in rodeo events such as bareback riding, bull dogging, and wild-cow milking.
www.angolarodeo.com

Baton Rouge Blues Week, Baton Rouge

Every September, Baton Rouge goes crazy for blues music. The festivities include movies, radio shows, and art shows about the blues; blues-inspired dishes at local restaurants; and, of course, live blues music.
www.festivalfinder.com/search/
details.cfm?eventid=USLAB51361

Black Heritage Festival, Lake Charles

Artists of all media come to Lake Charles for this two-day festival in March that

▲ Searching for Lafitte's treasure in Lake Charles.

celebrates African-American culture and community. Events include dance performances, live music, a beauty pageant, and a crafts show.
www.visitlakecharles.org/festival.asp

Cannes Brulee Powwow, Kenner

This annual festival celebrates Native American life in Louisiana with intertribal dance contests, storytelling, drumming, arts and crafts, and traditional foods.
For more information, call 504-468-7231.

Contraband Days, Lake Charles

Legend has it that Louisiana pirate Jean Lafitte buried treasure near Lake Charles. Every year, for two weeks in May, the city celebrates the riches of its history and culture with concerts, parades, sporting events, and a carnival.
www.contrabanddays.com

Crawfish Festival, Breaux Bridge

Each May, residents of Breaux Bridge welcome visitors to town to celebrate their delicious crawfish with live music, dance contests, crawfish-eating contests, and Cajun cooking demonstrations.
www.bbcrawfest.com

Festival International de Louisiane, Lafayette

Held the last week in April, this is the largest French-speaking festival in the United States. Events include live music by international artists, dancing, storytelling, plays, food, and arts and crafts.
www.festivalinternational.com

Festivals Acadiens, Lafayette

Every year in late September, the people of Lafayette celebrate Cajun life, food, and music with feasts and live music performances.
www.lafayettetravel.com/cfm/happenings/festivals/fest_aca.cfm

Jean Lafitte Seafood Festival, Lafitte

Enjoy a variety of seafood as well as games, rides, and local crafts at this annual community celebration held in August.
www.jeanlafittetours.com/calendar.htm

Louisiana Folklife Festival, Monroe

Gospel, blues, and zydeco artists perform at this annual festival in September, which also includes storytelling events, a fishing contest for kids, and cooking demonstrations.
www.louisianafolklifefest.org

Mamou Cajun Music Festival, Mamou

This two-day festival in September features live music, local food, and traditional competitions and entertainment such as pole climbing and boudin-eating contests. Experts teach fiddling, quilting, and Cajun dance.
www.asbank.com/~vpcoc/festivals/mcmf.htm

Mystic Krewe of Barkus Parade, New Orleans

Since 1993, canine residents of New Orleans have been able to celebrate Mardi Gras in their own way with a parade through the French Quarter, featuring costumes, small floats, and the crowning of a Queen and King of Barkus.
www.barkus.org

New Orleans Jazz and Heritage Festival, New Orleans

This famous weeklong event draws artists and audiences from all over the world to celebrate music and Louisiana culture. All kinds of music, from Dixieland jazz to contemporary rock, are performed live in venues throughout the city. The festival also incorporates a Native American celebration of music, film, and art.
www.nojazzfest.com

Pepper Festival, St. Martinville

Louisianans celebrate the hot peppers that give Cajun food its kick in this day-long party, which includes live music, Cajun food stalls, and a hot-pepper eating contest for the brave of tongue.
www.tabasco.com/taste_tent/festivals/oct_pepper_fest.cfm

Red River Revel Arts Festival, Shreveport

This big outdoor art festival features visual artists, musicians, and theater groups as well as food and crafts. A fishing tournament and regatta are also part of the fun.
www.redriverrevel.com

Southwest Louisiana Zydeco Festival, Opelousas

Come dance to the strains of half a dozen zydeco bands in this annual celebration of one of Louisiana's original art forms.
www.zydeco.org/index.html

▼ Music fans parade in their finery during the New Orleans Jazz and Heritage Festival.

Books

Bial, Raymond. *Cajun Home*. Boston: Houghton Mifflin, 1998. This book tells the story of Cajun history and daily life and includes many photographs.

Bridges, Ruby. *Through My Eyes*. New York: Scholastic, 1999. Ruby Bridges was the first African-American student to integrate the William Frantz School in New Orleans in 1960. She tells the story here of the difficulties she encountered and how she overcame them, in this important chapter in U.S. history.

Fahlenkamp-Merrell, Kindle. *Louis Armstrong (Journey to Freedom)*. Chanhassen, MN: Child's World, 2001. The exciting life story of Louis Armstrong — jazz pioneer, civil rights advocate, and New Orleans native — is told here.

Hintz, Martin, and Deborah Kent. *Louisiana (America the Beautiful)*. New York: Children's Press, 1998. Learn more interesting facts about Louisiana's past and present.

Moore, Elizabeth Butler, and Alice Couvillon. *Louisiana Indian Tales*. Gretna, LA: Pelican Publishing, 1990. This collection of traditional stories from Louisiana's Native Americans gives insight into their rich history and culture.

Vogt, Lloyd. *A Young Person's Guide to New Orleans Houses*. Gretna, LA: Pelican Pubishing, 1992. Tour historic New Orleans from your own home, or take this book along when you go to the Crescent City. The architecture of New Orleans reflects the many different influences on Louisiana culture.

Web Sites

▶ Official state web site
www.state.la.us

▶ State capital web site
www.ci.baton-rouge.la.us

▶ Louisiana Historical Society web site
www.louisianahistoricalsociety.org